Table of Contents

Unit 1 At School	page 2
Unit 2 My Things	page 10
Units 1–2 Listen and Review	page 18
Let's Learn About Numbers 20–100	page 19
Unit 3 My House	page 20
Unit 4 Things to Eat	page 28
Units 3–4 Listen and Review	page 36
Let's Learn About the Months	page 37
Unit 5 Occupations	page 38
Unit 6 Locations	page 44
Units 5–6 Listen and Review	page 54
Let's Learn About the Seasons	page 55
Unit 7 Doing Things	page 56
Unit 8 After School	page 64
Units 7–8 Listen and Review	page 72
Let's Learn About Time	page 73
Syllabus	page 74
Teacher and Student Card List	page 77
Word List	page 78

Hi, I'm Ginger!

Hi, I'm Sam!

Let's Start

Let's Learn

Let's Learn More

Let's Build

Units Review

Let's Learn About

Unit 1 At School

Let's Start

A. Let's talk.

B. Let's sing.

The Hello and Good-bye Song

Hi, Scott, how are you?
  I'm OK, thank you.
Hi, Scott, how are you?
  I'm OK, thank you.
Hi, Scott, how are you?
  I'm OK, thank you.
How about you?

Good-bye, Scott.
  See you later, alligator!
Good-bye, Scott.
  See you later, alligator!
Good-bye, Scott.
  See you later, alligator!
See you later, alligator!
Good-bye, Scott!

C. Let's move.

1. erase the board

2. speak English

3. write my name

4. read books

  I <u>erase the board</u> at school.

Unit 1 / At School

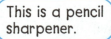
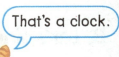

Let's Learn

A. Practice the words.

1. a pencil sharpener

2. a picture

3. a workbook

4. a paper clip

5. a clock

6. a door

7. a window

8. a calendar

B. Practice the sentences.

This is a pencil sharpener.
That's a clock.

That is = That's

4   Unit 1 / At School

C. Practice the questions and answers.

> What's this? What's that?
> It's a workbook. It's a calendar.

What is = What's
It is = It's

D. Ask and answer.

> Is this / that a calendar? Yes, it is.
>   No, it isn't.

is not = isn't

1.
2.
3.
4.
5.
6.

Unit 1 / At School

Let's Learn More

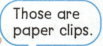

A. Practice the words.

1. pencil sharpeners

2. paper clips

3. clocks

4. workbooks

5. calendars

6. pictures

7. windows

8. doors

B. Practice the sentences.

These are pencil sharpeners.
Those are pictures.

C. Practice the questions and answers.

they are = they're

D. Ask and answer.

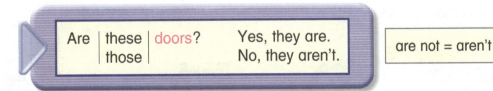

are not = aren't

1. 2. 3. 4.

Let's Build

A. Make sentences.

1.
2.
3.
4.

B. Say these.

1.
   new
2.
   round
3.
   old
4.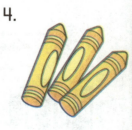
   yellow

C. Listen and check.

1.
   ☐ ☐ ☐ ☐

2.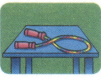
   ☐ ☐ ☐ ☐

3.
   ☐ ☐

4.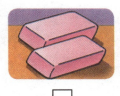
   ☐ ☐

D. Ask your partner.

1. Are those clocks square?
   ☐ Yes, they are.
   ☐ No, they aren't.

2. Are these crayons big?
   ☐ Yes, they are.
   ☐ No, they aren't.

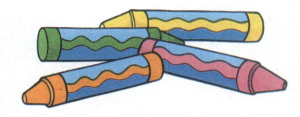

3. Is this ruler long?
   ☐ Yes, it is.
   ☐ No, it isn't.

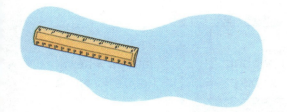

4. Is that window small?
   ☐ Yes, it is.
   ☐ No, it isn't.

Unit 1 / At School

Unit 2 My Things

 Let's Start

A. Let's talk.

B. Let's sing.

Whose Bag Is That?

Whose bag is that?
 I don't know.
Is it Scott's bag?
 No, no, no.
 It isn't his bag.
 No, it isn't.
 No, it isn't Scott's bag.

Is it Jenny's bag?
 Yes, it is.
 It's her bag.
 Yes, it is.
 It isn't his bag.
 It's her bag.
 It isn't Scott's bag.

C. Let's move.

1. run

2. swim

3. sing

4. dance

He / She can run.

Unit 2 / My Things

Let's Learn

A. Practice the words.

1. a key

2. a candy bar

3. a comic book

4. a comb

5. a coin

6. a brush

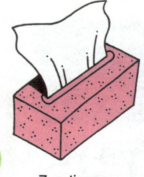
7. a tissue

8. a watch

B. Practice the sentence.

I have a key

C. Practice the question and answer.

D. Ask your partner.

Do you have a tissue? Yes, I do.
　　　　　　　　　　　No, I don't.

do not = don't

What does he have?

He has a camera.

Let's Learn More

A. Practice the words.

1. a camera

2. a key chain

3. a music player

4. a calculator

5. a train pass

6. an umbrella

7. a lunch box

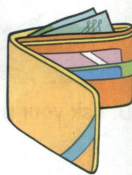
8. a wallet

B. Practice the sentence.

| He / She | has | a camera. |

Unit 2 / My Things

C. Practice the question and answer.

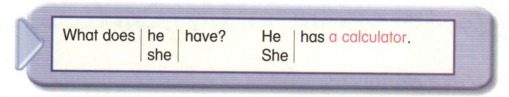

What does | he | have?   He | has a calculator.
         | she | She |

D. Ask and answer.

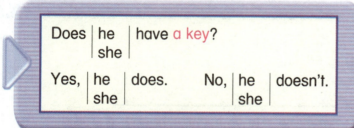

Does | he | have a key?
     | she |

Yes, | he | does.   No, | he | doesn't.
     | she | | she |

does not = doesn't

1.   2.

3.   4.

Let's Build

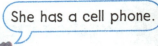

"He has a yo-yo."
"She has a cell phone."

A. Make sentences. CD 1 43

"He has a video game in his bag."
"She has a pencil in her bag."

B. Ask and answer. CD 1 44

| What does | he / she | have in | his / her | hand? |

He has a yo-yo in his hand.
She has a cell phone in her hand.

1.
2.
3.
4.

16 Unit 2 / My Things

C. Listen and check.

Does she have a candy bar in her bag?
　Yes, she does.
Does he have a calculator in his hand?
　No, he doesn't.

1. ☐ Yes, she does.
　☐ No, she doesn't.
2. ☐ Yes, he does.
　☐ No, he doesn't.
3. ☐ Yes, she does.
　☐ No, she doesn't.
4. ☐ Yes, he does.
　☐ No, he doesn't.
5. ☐ Yes, he does.
　☐ No, he doesn't.
6. ☐ Yes, she does.
　☐ No, she doesn't.

D. Ask your partner.

Do you have a _____ in your bag?

Yes					
No					

Unit 2 / My Things

Units 1-2 Listen and Review

Listen and circle. CD 1 46

1.
   a b c

2.
   a b c

3.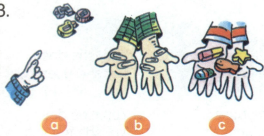
   a b c

4.
   a b c

5.
   a b c

6.
   a b c

7.
   a b

8.
   a b

18 Units 1-2 Listen and Review

Let's Learn About Numbers 20-100

Say these.

20 twenty

21 twenty-one

22 twenty-two

23 twenty-three

24 twenty-four

25 twenty-five

26 twenty-six

27 twenty-seven

28 twenty-eight

29 twenty-nine

30 thirty

40 forty

50 fifty

60 sixty

70 seventy

80 eighty

90 ninety

100 one hundred

Unit 3 My House

 Let's Start

A. Let's talk.

B. Let's sing.

Hillsdale

Where do you live?
In Hillsdale.
Where do you live?
In Hillsdale.
I live in Hillsdale.
How about you?
I live in Hillsdale, too.

What's your address
in Hillsdale?
What's your address
in Hillsdale?
It's North Street,
Number forty-two.
I live next to you!

C. Let's move.

1. play baseball

2. use chopsticks

3. ice-skate

4. do a magic trick

What can	he / she	do?	He / She	can play baseball

Let's Learn

A. Practice the words.

1. bed
2. bathtub
3. sofa
4. stove
5. lamp

6. sink
7. toilet
8. TV
9. refrigerator
10. telephone

B. Practice the sentence.

> There's a bed in the bedroom.

There is = There's

living room bedroom kitchen bathroom

C. Practice the question and answer.

Where's the sofa?
It's in the living room.

Where is = Where's
It is = It's

D. Ask and answer.

Is there a lamp in the bedroom?   Yes, there is.
                                  No, there isn't.

is not = isn't

1.
2.
3.
4.
5.

Let's Learn More

A. Practice the words.

1. next to
2. in front of
3. behind

B. Practice the sentences.

There's a lamp next to the sofa.

There are lamps behind the sofa.

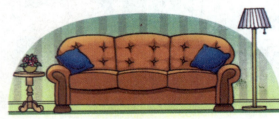 

1.
2.
3.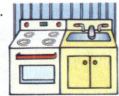
4.
5.
6.
7.
8.

C. Practice the question and answer.

| Is there a stove next to the sink? | Yes, there is.
No, there isn't. | is not = isn't |

D. Ask and answer.

| Are there lamps behind the bed? | Yes, there are.
No, there aren't. | are not = aren't |

1.
2.
3.

Let's Build

A. Ask and answer. (CD 1 - 68)

in
under
in front of
behind
next to

1. 2. 3. 4. 5.

B. Make two sentences. (CD 1 - 69)

There's a table in front of the sofa.
There's a sofa behind the table.

C. Listen and circle.

D. Let's sing.

Where Are the Books?

Where are the books?
   They're under the bed.
Where are the books?
   They're behind the sofa.
   They're on the table next to the chair.
   The books are everywhere!

Is there a book next to the door?
   Yes, there is.
Are there books on the floor?
   Yes, there are.
Are there books on the chair?
   Yes, there are, yes, there are—
   The books are everywhere!

Unit 4 Things To Eat

Let's Start

A. Let's talk. CD1 72

CD1 73 Do you want spaghetti?   Yes, please.
No, thank you!

B. Let's sing.

The Spaghetti Song

Do you like spaghetti?
  Yes, I do.
    I do, too.
      I do, too.
Do you like spaghetti?
  Yes, I do.
I like spaghetti, too!

Do you want spaghetti?
  Yes, I do.
    I do, too.
      I do, too.
Do you want spaghetti?
  Yes, I do.
I want spaghetti, too!

C. Let's move.

1. type

2. wink

3. do a cartwheel

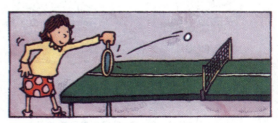
4. play Ping-Pong

| Can | he / she | type? | Yes, | he / she | can. | No, | he / she | can't. |

Unit 4 / Things to Eat

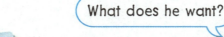
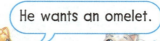

Let's Learn

A. Practice the words.

1. an omelet
2. a peach
3. a pear
4. a pancake

5. yogurt
6. cereal
7. tea
8. hot chocolate

B. Practice the sentences.

| He | wants | an omelet. |
| She | | yogurt. |

30 Unit 4 / Things to Eat

C. Practice the questions and answers.

| What does | he
she | want? | He
She | wants | a peach.
yogurt. |

1.
2.
3.
4.
5.
6.

D. Ask and answer.

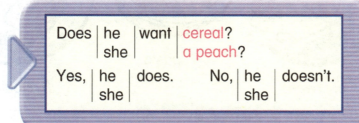

| Does | he
she | want | cereal?
a peach? |
| Yes, | he
she | does. | No, | he
she | doesn't. |

does not = doesn't

1.
2.
3.
4.

Unit 4 / Things to Eat

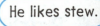

Let's Learn More

A. Practice the words.

1. grapes
2. pancakes
3. peaches
4. hamburgers
5. stew
6. cheese
7. pasta
8. steak

B. Practice the sentences.

| He | likes | grapes. |
| She | | stew. |

C. Practice the question and answer.

What does	he	like?	He	likes hamburgers.
	she		She	

D. Ask and answer.

Does	he	like stew?	Yes,	he	does.	No,	he	doesn't.
	she			she			she	

1.
2.
3.
4.

Unit 4 / Things to Eat 33

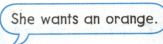

Let's Build

A. Choose the correct word.

1. ☐ likes
   ☐ wants

2. ☐ likes
   ☐ wants

3. ☐ likes
   ☐ wants

4. ☐ likes
   ☐ wants

B. Listen and circle.

1.
   a   b

2.
   a   b

3.
   a   b

4.
   a   b

34 Unit 4 / Things to Eat

C. Ask and answer.

> Does | he | want a pear or an orange?   He | wants an orange.
> | she | She |

1.
2.
3.
4.

D. Ask and answer.

> How many peaches does he want?
> He wants two peaches.

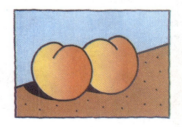

1. peaches 2. cookies 3. books 4. games 5. CDs

Unit 4 / Things to Eat

Units 3-4 Listen and Review

A. Listen and number.

B. Listen and circle.

1.
     a   b   c

2.
     a   b   c

3.
     a   b   c

4.
     a   b   c

5.
     a   b

6.
     a   b

Let's Learn About the Months

Make sentences. CD 1 / 97

What month is it?

It's January.

1. January

2. February

3. March

4. April

5. May

6. June

7. July

8. August

9. September

10. October

11. November

12. December

Unit 5 Occupations

Let's Start

A. Let's talk.

Who's she?
She's the new nurse.

Who is = Who's
She is = She's

B. Let's sing.

What's the Matter?

What's the matter?   What's the matter?
What's the matter?   Are you OK?
What's the matter?   I am sick today.
  I am sick.   Oh, no!

hot   cold   tired   sad

C. Let's move.

1. wake up

2. get out of bed

3. make breakfast

4. get dressed

  I wake up every morning.

Who's she?

She's Miss Wilson.
She's a shopkeeper.

Let's Learn

A. Practice the words.

1. a shopkeeper

2. a cook

3. a nurse

4. a farmer

5. a taxi driver

6. a train conductor

7. an office worker

8. a police officer

9. a teacher

10. a student

B. Practice the sentence.

| He's | a shopkeeper. |
| She's | |

Unit 5 / Occupations

C. Practice the questions and answers.

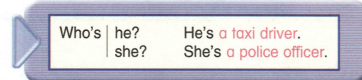

| Who's | he? | He's a taxi driver. |
| | she? | She's a police officer. |

Who is = Who's

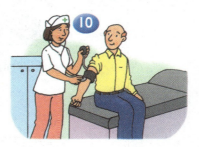

D. Ask and answer.

| Is | he | a farmer? | Yes, | he | is. | No, | he | isn't. |
| | she | | | she | | | she | |

1.    2.    3.    4.

Unit 5 / Occupations 41

Who are they?

They're Mr. and Mrs. Long. They're teachers.

Let's Learn More

A. Practice the words.

1. teachers

2. police officers

3. doctors

4. pilots

5. engineers

6. train conductors

7. firefighters

8. taxi drivers

9. students

10. dentists

B. Practice the sentence.

They're dentists.

They are = They're

42 Unit 5 / Occupations

C. Practice the question and answer.

1.
Ms. Adams and Mr. White

2. Mr. Gray and Ms. Johnson

3. Mr. and Mrs. Brown

4.
Mr. Baker and Mr. Simmons

D. Ask and answer.

Are they teachers?   Yes, they are.
                     No, they aren't.

1.
2.
3.

Unit 5 / Occupations

Let's Build

A. Listen and number.

B. Ask and answer.

Who is Mr. Jones?   He's a train conductor.

1. Mr. Jones
   train conductor

2. Miss Black
   teacher

3. Ms. Smith
   nurse

4. Mr. White
   pilot

5. Mr. Lee
   cook

C. Answer the questions.

Is Ms. Lee a teacher or a student?

She's a teacher.

1. Is Mr. Thomas a police officer or a train conductor?

2. Is Mrs. Hall an office worker or a teacher?

3. Is Ms. Baker a pilot or a doctor?

D. Ask your partner.

1. Can you make breakfast at school?
   ☐ Yes, I can.
   ☐ No, I can't.

2. Can the students dance at school?
   ☐ Yes, they can.
   ☐ No, they can't.

3. Can Mr. Green use chopsticks?
   ☐ Yes, he can.
   ☐ No, he can't.

4. Can Mrs. Hill play baseball?
   ☐ Yes, she can.
   ☐ No, she can't.

Unit 5 / Occupations

Unit 6 Locations

 **Let's Start**

A. Let's talk.

B. Let's sing.

Where's Tim?

Where's Tim?
  He's in the gym.
Where's Fred?
  He's home in bed.
Where's Anne?
  She's in Japan.
Where's Joe?
  I don't know!

Where are Jack and Jill?
  They're in Brazil.
Where's Lee?
  Under the apple tree.
Where's Gus?
  He's on the bus.
Where's Joe?
  I don't know!

C. Let's move.

1. study English

2. talk on the telephone

3. watch TV

4. practice the piano

What do you do every afternoon?
  I study English.

Unit 6 / Locations

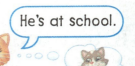

Let's Learn

A. Practice the words.

1. at school

2. at home

3. at work

4. at the library

5. at the park

6. at the zoo

B. Practice the sentence.

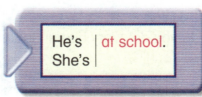

He's / She's at school.

Unit 6 / Locations

C. Practice the question and answer.

| Where is | he? | | He's | at the park. |
| | she? | | She's | |

D. Ask and answer.

| Is | he | at home? | Yes, | he | is. | No, | he | isn't. | He's | at school. |
| | she | | | she | | | she | | She's | |

1.
2.
3.

Where are they?

They're at the movies.

Let's Learn More

A. Practice the words.

1. at the movies

2. at the store

3. in the restaurant

4. on the bus

5. on the train

6. in the taxi

B. Practice the sentence.

They're at the movies.

C. Practice the question and answer.

> Where are they?   They're in the taxi.

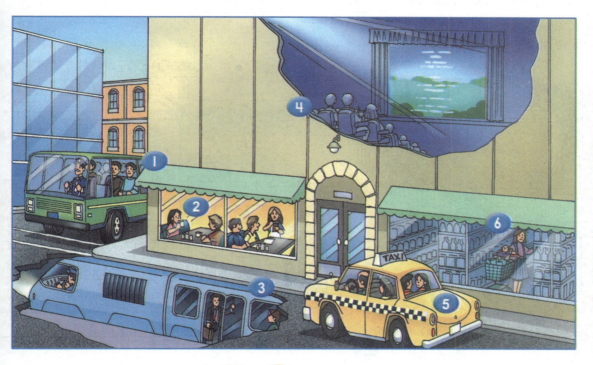

D. Ask and answer.

> Are they at the park?   Yes, they are.
>   No, they aren't.

1.
2.
3.

Let's Build

A. Make sentences. (CD 2, 44)

The shopkeeper is at the store.
The students are at school.

B. Ask and answer. (CD 2, 45)

Where's the cook? Where are the cooks?
He's in the kitchen. They're in the kitchen.

1.
2.
3.

C. Listen and circle.

D. Where are they?

Where's Ken?
He's on the chair.

Units 5-6 Listen and Review

A. Listen and circle.

1.
   a   b   c

2.
   a   b   c

3.
   a   b   c

4.
   a   b   c

5.
   a   b

6.
   a   b

B. Listen and number.

Let's Learn About the Seasons

Make sentences.

What can you do in the spring?

I can fly a kite.

1. spring
2. summer
3. fall
4. winter

Unit 7 Doing Things

Let's Start

A. Let's talk.

B. Let's sing.

Doing Things

What's he doing?
  Reading,
  He's reading
  He's reading.
What's he reading?
  He's reading a comic book and talking on the telephone.

What's she doing?
  Eating,
  She's eating,
  She's eating.
What's she eating?
  She's eating spaghetti and talking on the telephone.

What are you doing?
  Cooking,
  I'm cooking,
  I'm cooking.
What are you cooking?
  I'm cooking breakfast and talking on the telephone.

C. Let's move.

1. cook dinner

2. wash the dishes

3. read e-mail

4. do homework

Do you cook dinner every evening?
  Yes, I do.
  No, I don't.

Unit 7 / Doing Things 57

Let's Learn

A. Practice the words.

1. dancing

2. fishing

3. sleeping

4. coloring a picture

5. singing a song

6. running

7. walking

8. throwing a ball

B. Practice the sentence.

He's / She's dancing.

58 Unit 7 / Doing Things

C. Practice the question and answer.

What's | he / she | doing?   He's / She's | swimming.

D. Ask and answer.

Is | he / she | running?   Yes, | he / she | is.   No, | he / she | isn't.

1. Is he running?

2. Is she dancing?

3. Is she fishing?

4. Is he reading e-mail?

Unit 7 / Doing Things

What are they doing?

They're playing soccer.

Let's Learn More

A. Practice the words.

1. playing soccer

2. studying English

3. talking on the telephone

4. watching TV

5. reading comic books

6. riding bicycles

7. flying kites

8. eating apples

B. Practice the sentence.

They're playing soccer.

they're = they are

60 Unit 7 / Doing Things

C. Practice the question and answer.

> What are they doing?   They're singing a song.

1.
2.
3.
4.
5.
6.

D. Ask and answer.

> Are they doing homework?
> Yes, they are.
> No, they aren't. They're watching TV.

1.
2.
3.
4.

Let's Build

A. Make sentences.

She's walking.
They're throwing a ball.

he's
she's
they're

walk → walking
throw → throwing
listen → listening
do → doing

B. Ask your partner.

What are they doing?
They're sleeping.

1.
2.
3.
4.

C. Listen and check.

1. ☐ Yes, he is.
   ☐ No, he isn't.

2. ☐ Yes, they are.
   ☐ No, they aren't.

3. ☐ Yes, she is.
   ☐ No, she isn't.

4. ☐ Yes, he is.
   ☐ No, he isn't.

D. Ask your partner.

1. What's he eating?

2. What are they playing?

3. What's she reading?

4. What's he doing?

Unit 8 After School

Let's Start

A. Let's talk. CD2 71

CD2 72

Can you come over on Saturday?
 Yes, I can.
 Sorry. No, I can't. I'm busy.

B. Let's sing.

Can You Come Over?

Can you come over on Monday?
Can you come over on Monday?
　I can't come over on Monday.
　I'm very, very busy.

Can you come over on Tuesday?
Can you come over on Tuesday?
　I can't come over on Tuesday.
　I'm very, very busy.

　　Can you come over on Sunday?
　　Can you come over on Sunday?
　　　I can come over on Sunday.
　　　On Sunday I'm not busy.

C. Let's move.

1. take a walk

2. look at stars

3. play outside

4. take a bath

Do you ever take a walk at night?
　Yes, I do.
　No, I don't.

Unit 8 / After School

"What do you do on Mondays?"

"I go to art class."

Let's Learn

A. Practice the words.

1. art class

2. English class

3. math class

4. dance class

5. karate class

6. soccer practice

7. piano class

8. swimming class

B. Practice the sentence.

I go to art class.

C. Practice the question and answer.

What do you do on Mondays?
I go to dance class.

on Mondays = every Monday

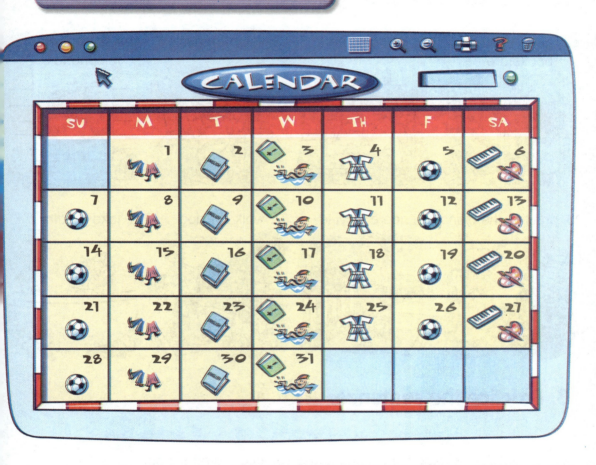

D. What about you?

What do you do on Saturdays?

I _____.

SATURDAY

Let's Learn More

"What does she do after school?"
"She goes to the bookstore."

A. Practice the words.

1. go to the bookstore

2. do homework

3. listen to music

4. talk on the telephone

5. practice the piano

6. ride a bicycle

7. walk the dog

8. take a bath

B. Practice the sentence.

He / She goes to the bookstore after school.

go → goes
do → does
listen → listens
talk → talks

practice → practices
ride → rides
walk → walks
take → takes

68 Unit 8 / After School

C. Practice the question and answer.

| What does | he / she | do after school? | He / She | goes to the bookstore. |

D. Ask and answer.

| Does | he / she | do homework after school? |
| Yes, | he / she | does. | No, | he / she | doesn't. |

1.
2.
3.
4.

Unit 8 / After School

She goes to her karate class after school.

Let's Build

A. Make sentences.

> I go to my English class after school.

1. English class
2. math class
3. dance class

4. swimming class
5. karate class
6. art class

B. Listen and check.

1. ☐ He goes to his English class.
   ☐ She goes to her English class.

2. ☐ She goes to her math class.
   ☐ He goes to his math class.

3. ☐ He goes to his karate class.
   ☐ She goes to her karate class.

4. ☐ He goes to his swimming class.
   ☐ She goes to her swimming class.

5. ☐ She goes to her art class.
   ☐ He goes to his art class.

6. ☐ She goes to her piano class.
   ☐ He goes to his piano class.

C. Ask and answer.

> What does he do on Tuesdays?
> He goes to his math class on Tuesdays.

1. What does he do on Tuesdays?
2. What does he do on Wednesdays?
3. What does he do on Saturdays?
4. What does she do on Thursdays?
5. What does she do on Mondays?
6. What does she do Fridays?

D. Ask your partner.

1. What do you do after school on Tuesdays?
2. Do you go to English class after school?

Units 7-8 Listen and Review

A. Listen and circle.

10. Thursday

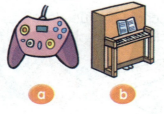

11. Friday

Let's Learn About Time

A. What time is it?

1.
3:00
three o'clock

2.
6:15
six fifteen

3.
8:30
eight thirty

4.
10:45
ten forty-five

B. Say these.

1.
It's 7:00 in the morning. It's 7:00 a.m.

2.
It's 4:25 in the afternoon. It's 4:25 p.m.

3.
It's 6:43 in the evening. It's 6:43 p.m.

4.
It's 9:52 at night. It's 9:52 p.m.

Let's Go 2 Syllabus

Unit 1   At School

Let's Start	Let's Learn	Let's Learn More	Let's Build
Hi, Scott. How are you? I'm OK, thanks. How about you? Pretty good! Good-bye, Scott. See you later! Saying hello and good-bye I erase the board at school. Describing school activities	This is a pencil sharpener. That's a clock. What's this/that? It's a workbook. Is this/that a calendar? Yes, it is./No, it isn't. Identifying and asking about near and far school objects (singular)	These/Those are pencil sharpeners. What are these/those? They're clocks. Are these/those doors? Yes, they are./No, they aren't. Identifying and asking about near and far school objects (plural)	This/that door is little/big. These/those clocks are new. Is that window small? Yes, it is./No, it isn't. Are those clocks square? Yes, they are. No, they aren't. Identifying near and far objects with adjectives

Unit 2   My Things

Let's Start	Let's Learn	Let's Learn More	Let's Build
Whose bag is that? I don't know. Is it Scott's bag? No, it isn't his bag. Is it Jenny's bag? Yes, it's her bag! Talking about possessions She can run. Describing ability	I have a key. Expressing possession What do you have? I have a coin. Do you have a tissue? Yes, I do./No, I don't. Asking about possessions	She has a camera. What does he have? He has a calculator. Does she have a key? Yes, she does. No, she doesn't. Identifying the possessions of others	He has a video game in his bag. What does she have in her hand? She has a yo-yo in her hand. Does she have a candy bar in her bag/hand? Yes, she does./No, she doesn't. Do you have a _ in your bag? Asking about possessions and expressing their locations

Units 1–2 Listen and Review   **Let's Learn About Numbers 20–100**
Counting

Unit 3   My House

Let's Start	Let's Learn	Let's Learn More	Let's Build
Where do you live, Jenny? I live in Hillsdale. What's your address? It's 16 North Street. What's your cell phone number? It's (798) 555-2043. Asking for and giving personal information What can he do? He can play baseball. Asking about ability	There's a bed in the bedroom. Where's the sofa? It's in the living room. Is there a stove in the bedroom? Yes, there is./No, there isn't. Clarifying locations of furniture (singular)	There's a lamp next to the sofa. There are lamps behind the sofa. Is there a stove next to the sink? Yes, there is./No, there isn't. Are there lamps behind the bed? Yes, there are./No, there aren't. Clarifying locations of furniture (singular and plural)	Where are the books? They're under the bed. There's a table in front of the sofa. There's a sofa behind the table. Where's the telephone? It's on the table next to the sofa. Is there a book next to the door?/Are there books on the floor? Asking and answering singular and plural questions about the locations of objects

Unit 4   Things to Eat

Let's Start
What's for lunch, Mom?
Spaghetti.
Mmm. That's good. I like spaghetti.
I do, too.
Do you want spaghetti?
Yes, please.
No, thank you!
Asking about and expressing wants and likes

Can he/she type?
Yes, he/she can.
No, he/she can't.
Asking about ability

Let's Learn
He wants an omelet/yogurt.

What does he want?
He wants a peach/yogurt.

Does she want cereal?
Yes, she does./No, she doesn't.
Asking about the wants of others (singular)

Let's Learn More
He likes grapes.

What does she like?
She likes hamburgers.

Does he like stew?
Yes, he does.
No, he doesn't.
Asking about the likes of others (singular)

Let's Build
He likes/wants hamburgers.

He doesn't want a dog. He wants a cat.
Expressing likes and wants

Does she want a pear or an orange?
She wants an orange.

How many peaches does he want?
He wants two peaches.
Asking about preferences and quantity

Units 3–4 Listen and Review

Let's Learn About the Months
What month is it?/It's January.

Unit 5   Occupations

Let's Start
What's the matter, Scott?
I'm sick.
That's too bad.
Maybe Mrs. Green can help you.
Who's she?
She's the new nurse.
Thanks for your help.
You're welcome. Get better soon!
Asking about someone's health

I wake up every morning.
Describing daily activities

Let's Learn
She's a shopkeeper.

Who's he?
He's a taxi driver.

Is she a farmer?
Yes, she is./No, she isn't.
Making statements and asking about occupations (singular)

Let's Learn More
They're dentists.

Who are they?
They're Mr. Jones and Mr. Lee. They're pilots.

Are they teachers?
Yes, they are.
No, they aren't.
Making statements and asking about people and occupations (plural)

Let's Build
I'm a nurse.

Who is Mr. Jones?
He's a train conductor.

Is Ms. Lee a teacher or a student?
She's a teacher.
Identifying self and people by occupation

Can Mrs. Hill play baseball?
Yes, she can.
No, she can't.
Asking about ability

Unit 6   Locations

Let's Start
Hi, Kate. This is Jenny.
Where are you?
I'm at home. Where are you?
I'm at the park. Can you come to the park?
Sure!
Determining location and making an invitation

What do you do every afternoon?
I study English.
Describing daily activities

Let's Learn
She's at school.

Where is she?
She's at the park.

Is he at home?
Yes, he is.
No, he isn't. He at school.
Expressing and asking about locations of people (singular)

Let's Learn More
They're at the movies.

Where are they?
They're in the taxi.

Are they at the park?
Yes, they are.
No, they aren't.
Expressing and asking about locations of people (plural)

Let's Build
The shopkeeper is at the store. The students are at school.

Where's the taxi driver?
She's in the taxi.
Where are the students?
They're at the store.

Is the teacher at the zoo?
Yes, he is./No, he isn't. He's at the store.
Are the students on the train?
Yes, they are./No, they aren't. They're at the library.
Clarifying occupations and locations of people (singular and plural)

Let's Go 2 Syllabus

Units 5–6 Listen and Review	Let's Learn About the Seasons
	What can you do in the spring?/I can fly a kite.

Unit 7   Doing Things

Let's Start	Let's Learn	Let's Learn More	Let's Build
Let's play a game! What are you doing? I'm riding a bicycle. What are you doing? We're swimming. *Asking what someone is doing*	She's dancing. What's she doing? She's swimming. Is he running? Yes, he is. / No, he isn't. *Asking about what others are doing (singular)*	They're playing soccer. What are they doing? They're singing a song. Are they doing homework? Yes, they are. No, they aren't. They're watching TV. *Asking about what others are doing (plural)*	She's walking. They're throwing a ball. What are they doing? They're sleeping. Is he doing a cartwheel? Yes, he is./No, he isn't. What is she eating? What are they playing? *Expressing and asking about what people are doing (singular and plural)*
Do you cook dinner every evening? Yes, I do./No, I don't. *Asking about frequency of daily activities*			

Unit 8   After School

Let's Start	Let's Learn	Let's Learn More	Let's Build
Can you come over on Saturday? Sorry. No, I can't. I'm busy. What about Sunday? Sunday is OK. I'm free. Great! See you on Sunday! OK. See you then! *Making plans and invitations*	I go to art class. What do you do on Mondays? I go to dance class. *Expressing and asking about after-school activities*	He goes to the bookstore after school. What does she do after school? She goes to the bookstore. Does he do homework after school? Yes, he does./No, he doesn't. *Expressing and asking about daily activities*	I go to my English class after school. He goes to his English class after school. What does he do on Tuesdays? He goes to his math class on Tuesdays. *Clarifying after-school activities*
Do you ever take a walk at night? Yes, I do./No, I don't. *Asking about frequency of daily activities*			

Units 7–8 Listen and Review	Let's Learn About Time
	What time is it?/It's 3:00.

76   Let's Go 2 Syllabus

Teacher and Student Card List Level Two

#		#		#		#	
1	erase the board	52	40/forty	103	March	154	in the taxi
2	speak English	53	50/fifty	104	April	155	spring
3	write my name	54	60/sixty	105	May	156	summer
4	read books	55	70/seventy	106	June	157	fall
5	a pencil sharpener	56	80/eighty	107	July	158	winter
6	a picture	57	90/ninety	108	August	159	cook dinner
7	a workbook	58	100/one hundred	109	September	160	wash dishes
8	a paper clip	59	play baseball	110	October	161	read e-mail
9	a clock	60	use chopsticks	111	November	162	do homework
10	a door	61	ice-skate	112	December	163	evening
11	a window	62	do a magic trick	113	wake up	164	dancing
12	a calendar	63	bed	114	get out of bed	165	fishing
13	pencil sharpeners	64	bathtub	115	make breakfast	166	sleeping
14	paper clips	65	sofa	116	get dressed	167	coloring a picture
15	clocks	66	stove	117	morning	168	singing a song
16	workbooks	67	lamp	118	a shopkeeper	169	running
17	calendars	68	sink	119	a cook	170	walking
18	pictures	69	toilet	120	a nurse	171	throwing a ball
19	windows	70	TV	121	a farmer	172	playing soccer
20	doors	71	refrigerator	122	a taxi driver	173	studying English
21	run	72	telephone	123	a train conductor	174	talking on the telephone
22	swim	73	living room	124	an office worker	175	watching TV
23	sing	74	bedroom	125	a police officer	176	reading comic books
24	dance	75	kitchen	126	a teacher	177	riding bicycles
25	a key	76	bathroom	127	a student	178	flying kites
26	a candy bar	77	next to	128	teachers	179	eating apples
27	a comic book	78	in front of	129	police officers	180	take a walk
28	a comb	79	behind	130	doctors	181	look at stars
29	a coin	80	spaghetti	131	pilots	182	play outside
30	a brush	81	type	132	engineers	183	take a bath
31	a tissue	82	wink	133	train conductors	184	night
32	a watch	83	do a cartwheel	134	firefighters	185	art class
33	a camera	84	play Ping-Pong	135	taxi drivers	186	English class
34	a key chain	85	an omelet	136	students	187	math class
35	a music player	86	a peach	137	dentists	188	dance class
36	a calculator	87	a pear	138	study English	189	karate class
37	a train pass	88	a pancake	139	talk on the telephone	190	soccer practice
38	an umbrella	89	yogurt	140	watch TV	191	piano class
39	a lunch box	90	cereal	141	practice the piano	192	swimming class
40	a wallet	91	tea	142	afternoon	193	go to the bookstore
41	20/twenty	92	hot chocolate	143	at school	194	do homework
42	21/twenty-one	93	grapes	144	at home	195	listen to music
43	22/twenty-two	94	pancakes	145	at work	196	talk on the telephone
44	23/twenty-three	95	peaches	146	at the library	197	practice the piano
45	24/twenty-four	96	hamburgers	147	at the park	198	ride a bicycle
46	25/twenty-five	97	stew	148	at the zoo	199	walk the dog
47	26/twenty-six	98	cheese	149	at the movies	200	take a bath
48	27/twenty-seven	99	pasta	150	at the store	201	three o'clock
49	28/twenty-eight	100	steak	151	in the restaurant	202	six fifteen
50	29/twenty-nine	101	January	152	on the bus	203	eight thirty
51	30/thirty	102	February	153	on the train	204	ten forty-five

Word List

A
a 4
a.m. 73
about 2
address 20
after 68
afternoon 47
alligator 3
am 2
an 14
apples 60
apple tree 47
April 37
are 2
aren't 7
art 66
at 3
August 37

B
bad 38
bag 10
ball 58
baseball 21
bath 65
bathroom 22
bathtub 22
bed 22
bedroom 22
behind 24
better 38
bicycle 56
big 8
board 3
books 3
bookstore 68
breakfast 39
brush 12
bus 47
busy 64

C
calculator 14
calendar 4
camera 14
can 11
can't 29
candy bar 12
cartwheel 29
cell phone 16
cereal 30
chair 27
cheese 32
chopsticks 21
class 66
clock 4
clocks 6
coin 12
cold 39
coloring 58
comb 12
come 46
comic book 12
cook 40
cooking 57

D
dance 11
dancing 58
December 37
dentists 42
dinner 57
dishes 57
do 12
doctors 42
does 14
doesn't 15
dog 68
doing 56
don't 10
door 4

E
eating 60
eighty 19
e-mail 57
engineers 42
English 3
erase 3
evening 57
every 39
everywhere 27

F
fall 55
farmer 40
February 37
fifty 19
firefighters 42
fishing 58
floor 27
flying 60
for 28
forty 19
free 64
Friday 72

G
get 38
get dressed 39
go 66
goes 68
good 2
good-bye 2
grapes 32
great 64
gym 47

H
hamburgers 32
has 14
have 12
he 11
he's 40
help 38
her 10
hi 2
his 10
home 46

homework 57
hot 39
hot chocolate 30
how 2

I
I 2
I'm 2
ice-skate 21
in 16
in front of 24
is 4
isn't 5
it 5
it's 5

J
January 37
July 37
June 37

K
karate class 66
key 12
key chain 14
kitchen 22
kites 60
know 10

L
lamp 22
later 2
let's 56
library 48
like 28
listen 68
listening 62
little 8
live 20
living room 22
long 9
look at 65
lunch 28
lunch box 14

M
magic trick 21
make 39
many 35
March 37
math 66
matter 38
May 37
maybe 38
mom 28
Monday 65
month 37
morning 39
movies 50
music 68
music player 14
my 3

N
name 3
new 8
next to 21
night 65
ninety 19
no 5
not 5
November 37
number 20
nurse 38

O
o'clock 73
October 37
office worker 40
OK 2
old 8
omelet 30
on 47
one hundred 19
or 35
out of 39
outside 65
over 64

P
p.m. 73
pancake 30
paper clip 4
park 46
pasta 32
peach 30
peaches 32
pear 30
pencil 16
pencil sharpener 4
piano 47
picture 4
pilots 42
Ping-Pong 29
play 21
playing 60
please 28
police officer 40
practice 47
pretty 2

R
read 3
reading 57
refrigerator 22
restaurant 50
rides 68
riding 56
round 8
rulers 8
run 11
running 58

S
sad 39
Saturday 64

school 3
seasons 55
see 2
September 37
seventy 19
she 11
she's 38
shopkeeper 40
sick 38
sing 11
singing 58
sink 22
sixty 19
sleeping 58
small 9
soccer 60
sofa 22
song 58
soon 38
sorry 64
spaghetti 28
speak 3
spring 55
square 9
stars 65
steak 32
stew 32
store 50
stove 22
student 40
study 47
studying 60
summer 55
Sunday 64
sure 46
swim 11
swimming 56

T
table 26
take 65
talk 47
talking 57
taxi 50
taxi driver 40
tea 30
teacher 40
telephone 22
thank you 28
thanks 2
that 4
that's 4
the 3
then 64
there 22
there's 22
these 6
they 7
they're 7
thirty 19
this 4
those 6
throwing 58
Thursday 72
time 73
tired 39

tissue 12
to 46
today 39
toilet 22
too 28
train 50
train conductor 40
train pass 14
Tuesday 65
TV 22
twenty 19
two 35
type 29

U
umbrella 14
under 26
use 21

V
very 65
video game 16

W
wake up 39
walk 65
walking 58
wallet 14
want 28
wash 57
watch 12
watch 47
watching 60
we're 56
Wednesday 72
welcome 38
what 5
what's 5
where 20
where's 22
who 38
who's 38
whose 10
window 4
wink 29
winter 55
work 48
workbook 4
write 3

Y
yellow 8
yes 5
yogurt 30
you 2
you're 38
your 17
yo-yo 16

Z
zoo 48